GETTING OLDER HUMOR

IRENE XANDERENA

GETTING OLDER HUMOR

ISBN: 979-8-8690-8504-7

Published by
Eyereneeswords
Email: life@eyereneeswords.com
Website: www.eyereneeswords.com

CONTENT

ACKNOWLEDGMENT

First and foremost, I would like to express my immense gratitude to my dear friend and partner in crime, "Time." Thank you for always reminding me of your presence and ensuring that I never forget about the ticking clock and the inevitable march of years. Your relentless pursuit of forward motion has certainly provided me with plenty of material for this book!

I must also extend my heartfelt appreciation to "Gravity," for keeping me grounded and reminding me that I can no longer bounce back from falls and mishaps as effortlessly as I once did. Your witty sense of humor, though sometimes painful, has certainly provided moments of comedic relief throughout the process of writing this book.

A special shout-out goes to my favorite pair of glasses, without which I would have surely mistyped countless words and misread many hilarious autocorrects. Your ability to magnify life's little details has truly been a sight for sore eyes. I owe a debt of gratitude to all the stubborn gray hairs that have sprouted on my head, dramatically highlighting my journey into the realm of "distinguished maturity." Your tenacity and refusal to be plucked have been a constant reminder that aging is not just a number, but a colorful badge of honor.

I am indebted to all the self-help books and anti-aging creams that have graced my shelves throughout the writing of this book. While your promises of eternal youth may be a tad exaggerated, your presence has certainly provided me with a good laugh and a reminder to embrace the natural process of aging with grace and humor.

This book is a tribute to the beauty, resilience, and wisdom that can be found in the later chapters of our lives. Let this book be a reminder that aging is not a solitary path, but a collective experience shared by countless individuals who have walked this road before us. Lastly, I would like to express my sincere appreciation to my family and friends who have gracefully put up with my aging-related rants, grumbles, and forgetfulness. Your endless patience and ability to laugh along with me have been a constant source of inspiration and support.

To all those who have played a part, big or small, in the creation of this book, I offer my heartfelt thanks. Your contributions, intentional or otherwise, have made this journey of getting older a truly hilarious and memorable one. With laughter and gratitude,

Irene Xanderena

INTRODUCTION

A Wrinkle in Time, and Gravity, and Glasses, Oh My! Welcome, fellow adventurers, to the wild and wacky world of getting older! Now, hold on tight to your reading glasses and prepare to embark on a journey filled with laughter, wisdom, and a few extra wrinkles. They say that with age comes wisdom, but they forget to mention the onslaught of peculiar happenings and unexpected surprises that accompany it.

As we navigate the uncharted territory of our golden years, we find ourselves facing a cast of characters that would make even the most imaginative novelist blush with envy. Aging is an inevitable and universal part of life. It is a journey that we all embark upon, filled with both joy and challenges. As the years pass, we witness the ever-changing landscape of our bodies, minds, and relationships.

First, let's talk about Time. That sneaky little scoundrel has a knack for playing tricks on us, doesn't it? One moment, we're young and carefree, and the next, we're hunting for our car keys and forgetting why we walked into a room. Time has a peculiar sense of humor, reminding us that we can't turn back its hands or pause its relentless march.

But fear not, my friends, for in this book, we shall learn to laugh in the face of Time and embrace the absurdity of its passing. And who can forget our dear friend Gravity? Oh, Gravity, you cheeky rascal! It seems that with each passing year, you become more determined to keep us grounded, sometimes quite literally. Suddenly, a simple trip to tie our shoelaces becomes a grand performance of balancing acts, wobbling, and praying that no one is watching. But hey, at least our falls provide endless entertainment for the younger generation, right?

Of course, we mustn't overlook the star of the show – our trusty sidekick, Glasses. Ah, Glasses, the unsung heroes of aging! They perch delicately on our noses, magnifying the small print and transforming us into wise scholars, or at least that's what we like to believe. But let's face it, they're also a constant reminder that our eyesight has decided to rebel, leaving us squinting and searching for our misplaced spectacles. Who knew that reading menus would become an adventure requiring advanced optical equipment?

As we embark on this journey together, we shall encounter other quirky characters, like those stubborn gray hairs that sprout defiantly from our heads, reminding us that we are earning our stripes of wisdom, one follicle at a time. But fear not, my friends, for in the midst of these comical misadventures, there is a beauty to be found. With each laugh line etched upon our faces, we gain stories to tell, memories to cherish, and a unique perspective on life that only age can provide. So let us embrace the quirks, the foibles, and the uncontrollable laughter that comes with getting older.

So, buckle up and prepare for a wild and hilarious ride through the ups and downs of the aging process. Together, we shall navigate the twists and turns, armed with humor and a healthy dose of self-deprecation. Let's face it – getting older may have its challenges, but when we can laugh at ourselves, we truly become timeless.

PREFACE

"May your laughter be contagious; your wrinkles be badges of honor and your heart be forever young."
@ Irene Xanderena

Dear reader, Welcome to the preface of a book that promises to take you on a hilarious journey through the trials and tribulations of getting older. You may be wondering why on earth I decided to write a humor book about such a topic. Well, let's face it, if we can't laugh at ourselves, we might as well hang up our reading glasses and retire to a life of knitting and crossword puzzles. Getting older is not exactly a trending topic on social media or the subject of glamorous Hollywood Films, but I will say it is like a roller coaster ride, filled with unexpected twists and turns and a few questionable choices in fashion along the way.

As we venture into our golden years, we find ourselves facing a myriad of challenges. Our bodies seem to develop a mind of their own engaging in rebellious acts such as popping joints and refusing to cooperate with our once reliable metabolism. This book is not a lamentation or a pity party; it is a celebration of the absurdity that comes with the passage of time. It is a reminder that life is meant to be lived, laughed at, and cherished, no matter how many wrinkles or gray hairs we accumulate along the way.

So, buckle up, my friends, and prepare for a wild ride filled with laughter, a few tears (from laughing too hard, of course), and a newfound appreciation for the incredible comedy that is getting older. Together, let's navigate this uncharted territory armed with humor, grace, and the occasional groan as we stand up from a chair. Thank you for joining me on this adventure.

Now, let's dive into the book and discover the wonders that await us as we embrace the hilarity of growing older so join me on this journey as we read "getting older humor!"

GETTING OLDER HUMOR

1

I've finally discovered the secret to eternal youth: lying about my age!

2

As I get older, my mind may be a little slower, but my ability to find the TV remote in random places has reached an expert level!

3

Getting older is like a game of hide-and-seek, except now it's my glasses that are hiding and my memory that's seeking!

4

Growing old is like a rollercoaster ride, except the only loops you experience are the loops of repeating yourself!

5

Getting older is like a game of hide and seek, but the only thing hiding is your car keys!

6

I used to have a six-pack, but now I have a keg... in the fridge!

7

As I grow older, I've noticed my memory is like a playlist on shuffle mode, always skipping the important stuff!

8

They say age is just
a number, but in my
case, that number is the
wrong password!

9

You know you're getting older when you bend down to tie your shoes and wonder what else you can do while you're down there.

10

I was told that with age comes wisdom, but all I seem to have acquired is a vast collection of random knowledge about TV shows from the '80s.

11

I've reached that age where my mind says, 'Go for it,' but my body says 'Sit down and take a nap.'

12

They say laughter is the best medicine, which explains why I'm constantly cracking up... my back!

13

At this point in life, my exercise routine consists of just trying to get up from the couch without making any weird noises.

14

I used to be able to pull an all-nighter, now I can barely pull off a mid-afternoon nap.

15

Growing older is like a never-ending story, except instead of dragons and magic, it's filled with doctor appointments and insurance forms!

16

I used to think my joints were made of rubber, but now I'm convinced they're made of creaky door hinges.

17

Getting older is like a never-ending game of 'Guess Who?' because half the time I can't recognize the people I used to know.

18

I used to stay up all night partying, now I stay up all night worrying about staying up all night.

19

My idea of a wild night out now involves staying up past 9 p.m. and having a second cup of decaf coffee.

20

I never thought I'd say this, but I'm looking forward to receiving socks as a birthday gift!

21

I used to bounce back from injuries like a rubber ball, now I bounce back like a deflated balloon.

22

I'm at the age where I can't remember if I'm having a 'senior moment' or if I just forgot what I was doing.

23

I've realized that my body is now a lot like my smartphone - it takes longer to charge and drains faster.

24

My memory used to be like a steel trap, now it's more like a sieve made of Swiss cheese.

25

I used to be able to party all night, now I'm lucky if I can make it past 9 p.m. without falling asleep.

26

I've finally reached the age where my back goes out more often than I do.

27

I used to think I was indecisive, but now I'm not so sure.

28

The only thing getting a workout these days is my credit card from all the supplements and vitamins.

29

I've come to accept that wrinkles are just love notes from life, but I could do without the love handles.

30

I used to dream of traveling the world, now I dream of a full night's sleep without any interruptions.

31

I've mastered the art of making 'old people noises' when I stand up, sit down, or do anything remotely physical.

32

I'm starting to believe that 'the golden years' refers to the color of my teeth.

33

You know you're getting older when you start using more emojis in your text messages to compensate for your declining eyesight.

34

I used to be able to eat whatever I wanted, now I just look at a slice of cake and gain five pounds.

35

My idea of a wild night out is staying up past 10 p.m. and indulging in a third cup of herbal tea.

36

I've discovered that the key to aging gracefully is investing in a good pair of elastic waistband pants.

37

I used to be able to multitask like a pro, now I struggle to remember what I was doing before I got distracted.

38

You know you're getting older when "getting lucky" means finding your car keys on the first try.

39

I'm at the age where I can't remember if it's my joints popping or the sound of applause for getting out of a chair.

40

I've realized that life is too short to worry about the number of candles on my birthday cake. Just bring out the cake!

41

You know you're getting older when you choose your breakfast cereal based on its fiber content rather than its taste.

42

I used to be able to pull an all-nighter, now I can't even pull off a decent comb-over.

43

I've reached the point where my idea of a 'quick recovery' is being able to get out of bed without making any weird noises.

44

Oh boy! I remember when emojis were just called 'hieroglyphics'.

45

You know you're getting older when your favorite playlist is called 'Songs That Make Me Feel Young'.

46

You know you're getting older when you receive a brochure for retirement homes and think, "Hmm, this actually looks pretty nice."

47

My joints are so noisy, that I could probably start a one-person band.

48

I used to be 'with it,' but then they changed what 'it' was. Now, what I'm 'with' isn't 'it,' and what's 'it' seems weird and scary to me.

49

It's amazing how a simple sneeze can make you question your entire pelvic floor.

50

I've reached the age where my knees crack more than a safe in a bank heist movie.

51

Remember when 'getting lucky' meant finding a parking spot? Ah, simpler times.

52

I used to think 'Netflix and chill' meant watching a movie with a bowl of ice cream. Now, I need a blanket and a cup of tea for that kind of excitement.

53

You know you're getting older when "all-nighter" means not having to get up to use the bathroom.

54

My favorite exercise now is 'running late'. It really gets my heart racing.

55

You know you're getting older when you can remember using a typewriter but still struggle with autocorrect.

56

My memory is so bad, I can hide my own Easter eggs and never find them.

57

I've come to realize that naps are not just for toddlers and cats – they're for the wise and tired too.

58

I'm at the age where going to bed early is a treat, and I don't even need an excuse.

59

You know you're getting older when you start every sentence with 'Back in my day...'

60

You know you're getting older when you're tempted to buy a rocking chair because it looks comfortable, not because it's trendy.

61

I'm starting to think that 'age is just a number' was invented by someone who can't count very well.

62

I've reached the point where I need a GPS to find my glasses, even when they're on top of my head.

63

You know you're getting older when your social media feed is filled with pictures of your friends' grandchildren instead of party pictures.

64

I used to think wrinkles added character, but now I realize they're just roadmaps of where my face has been.

65

Turning older is like a walk in the park. Jurassic Park.

66

I remember when a 'scroll' was something you did with a piece of paper, not on a computer screen.

67

I used to think a 'hot flash' was just the thermostat acting up, but now I know it's my body's way of saying, 'Surprise, you're on fire!'

68

I'm at the age where I can hurt myself sleeping. You should see the acrobatics I do just to roll over.

69

You know you're getting older when you have a designated "comfy chair" and getting up from it becomes a well-thought-out plan.

70

I used to be able to eat a whole pizza by myself. Now, just reading the menu gives me heartburn.

71

You know you're getting older when you have more candles on your birthday cake than friends at the party.

72

I've realized that 'adulting' doesn't mean having it all figured out; it just means pretending that you do.

73

I used to think my parents were overreacting about everything. Now, I realize they were just practicing for when I became a parent.

74

I've reached the age where my 'social calendar' is just a reminder to pay my bills on time.

75

You know you're getting older when you can't remember the last time you did something for the first time.

76

I’ve learned that ‘retail therapy’ is just a fancy term for ‘blowing my savings on things I don’t need.

77

I'm so old, I remember when the internet had to dial up and make weird noises. Ah, the good old days of waiting for a single web page to load.

78

I used to have a waistline, now I have a 'wine' line. It's a sign of maturity, right?

79

I remember when my joints were as quiet as a library. Now, they sound like a bowl of Rice Krispies.

80

I've reached an age where my favorite part of the newspaper is the obituaries. It's like a daily reminder to appreciate being alive.

81

I've realized that my memory is like a browser with too many tabs open. It crashes at the most inconvenient times.

82

You know you're getting older when you trade in your bucket list for a 'fuck-it' list.

83

You know you're getting older when you start receiving more birthday cards from your doctor than from your friends

84

I used to look forward to Friday nights for parties. Now, I look forward to Friday nights for a good night's sleep.

85

I've reached the age where my idea of a wild night is staying up past my bedtime.

86

You know you're getting older when you start using words like 'fancy' and 'digestion' in regular conversation.

87

You know you're getting older when you become a human weather forecast. 'My knee says it's going to rain, and my hip predicts a thunderstorm.

88

I've reached the age where my favorite part of going out is coming back home.

89

They say laughter is the best medicine, but at this age, we need all the medicine we can get just to laugh without throwing out our backs.

90

The best part about getting older is that you can finally say whatever you want because most of your friends can't hear you anyway!

91

Aging is like a roller coaster ride. It has its ups and downs and sometimes you just want to scream!

92

You know you are getting older when your anxieties shift from wondering if you look cute during your date to wondering if you turned off the stove before leaving the house.

93

They say time heals all wounds but as you get older you worry about what wicked pains time has planned for you down the years.

94

As you get older, you worry less about fitting in with the crowd and worry more about fitting into your pants after dinner.

95

They say laughter is the best medicine, but many have mistaken my crackling laughter for a medical emergency.

10 BENEFITS OF GETTING OLDER

1. **Wisdom:** With age comes experience and wisdom. You've accumulated a lifetime of knowledge and can offer valuable insights to others.
2. **Self-Acceptance:** As you age, you become more comfortable in your own skin. You have a better understanding of who you are and what truly matters to you.
3. **Appreciation for the Simple Things:** Getting older allows you to appreciate the little joys in life. A beautiful sunset, a warm cup of tea, or a heartfelt conversation become cherished moments.
4. **Stronger Relationships:** As time goes by, you learn to prioritize the relationships that truly

matter. You invest in deeper connections and create lasting bonds with loved ones.

5. **Freedom from Insecurities:** With age, you tend to care less about what others think of you. You embrace your quirks and imperfections, freeing yourself from self-doubt and insecurities.
6. **Increased Confidence:** As you face challenges and overcome obstacles throughout life, your confidence grows. You become more self-assured and better equipped to tackle new endeavors.
7. **Time for Pursuing Passions:** With retirement or a reduced workload, you have more time to dedicate to hobbies, interests, and passions that may have taken a backseat in earlier years.
8. **Perspective on Life:** Getting older offers a broader perspective on life. You realize that setbacks and disappointments are temporary

and that life's true joys lie in the moments and connections you make.

9. **Reduced FOMO (Fear of Missing Out):** As you age, you become more content with where you are and what you have. You no longer feel the need to constantly chase after the latest trends or keep up with everyone else.
10. **Embracing the Present:** Aging teaches you the importance of living in the present moment. You learn to savor each day, as you understand that time is a precious gift not to be wasted. Remember, getting older is not a burden but an opportunity for growth, self-discovery, and a life filled with laughter and joy. Embrace the journey and enjoy all the benefits that come with it!

10 WORDS OF WISDOM FROM PEOPLE AGED 50-69

1. "Embrace change, for it is through change that we grow and evolve."

2. "Life is too short to hold grudges; forgive and let go."

3. "Invest time in nurturing relationships, as they are the true wealth of life."

4. "Take care of your health, for without it, nothing else truly matters."

5. "Don't be afraid to take risks and pursue your passions; it's never too late to start."

6. “Find joy in the simple things; they often hold the greatest beauty.”

7. “Live with gratitude and appreciate the blessings that surround you.”

8. “Learn to listen more than you speak; wisdom often comes from silent observation.”

9. “Don’t underestimate the power of self-reflection and personal growth.”

10. “Remember that aging is just another chapter in the book of life, so make it a memorable one.”

10 WORDS OF WISDOM FROM PEOPLE AGED 70-89

1. "Cherish every day, for time becomes more precious as we age."

2. "Stay curious and continue to learn; knowledge has no age limit."

3. "Savor the present moment; it's where true happiness resides."

4. "Acceptance and contentment are the keys to inner peace."

5. "Prioritize experiences over possessions; memories are invaluable treasures."

6. "Nurture your spirit and embrace a positive outlook on life."

7. "Embrace solitude and find comfort in your own company."

8. "Share your wisdom with the younger generation; your voice matters."

9. "Seek beauty in the small details; it's often the overlooked that holds magic."

10. "Remember, you are never too old to dream and pursue new passions."

10 WORDS OF WISDOM FROM PEOPLE OVER 90 YEARS OLD

1. "Life is a journey, so enjoy the ride till the end."
2. "Adaptability is the key to navigating the challenges of aging."
3. "Gratitude is the secret to finding joy in every moment."
4. "Give love freely; it multiplies and brings immense fulfillment."
5. "Embrace change; it keeps the spirit alive and vibrant."

6. "Patience and resilience are the companions of longevity."

7. "Stay connected to loved ones; they are your greatest treasure."

8. "Laugh often; it's the elixir for a youthful heart."

9. "Simplify your life and find contentment in the little things."

10. "Leave a legacy of kindness; it's the true measure of a life well-lived."

www.ingramcontent.com/pod-product-compliance
Lightning Source LLC
Chambersburg PA
CBHW041333120726
48005CB00014B/2235